THE CHIRU
OF HIGH TIBET

THE CHIRU
OF HIGH TIBET

A TRUE STORY

written by Jacqueline Briggs Martin

illustrated by Linda Wingerter

HOUGHTON MIFFLIN BOOKS FOR CHILDREN
HOUGHTON MIFFLIN HARCOURT
BOSTON NEW YORK 2010

For my family,
who are part of all the journeys.
—J. B. M.

For Grace Lin and in memory of Robert Mercer.
—L. W.

Text copyright © 2010 by Jacqueline Briggs Martin
Illustrations copyright © 2010 by Linda Wingerter

The text of this book is set in Truesdell.
The illustrations were painted with acrylics.
Map illustration by Stephanie Cooper

Library of Congress Cataloging-in-Publication Data
Martin, Jacqueline Briggs.
The chiru of High Tibet / written by Jacqueline Briggs Martin ; illustrated by Linda Wingerter.
p. cm.
Includes bibliographical references.
ISBN 978-0-618-58130-6
1. Chiru—China—Tibet—Juvenile literature. 2. Chang Tang Plateau (China)—Description and travel
—Juvenile literature. 3. Schaller, George B.—Travel—China—Tibet—Juvenile literature.
I. Wingerter, Linda S., ill. II. Title.
QL737.U53M2274 2010
599.64—dc22
2009049

Printed in Singapore
TWP 10 9 8 7 6 5 4 3 2 1
4500228160

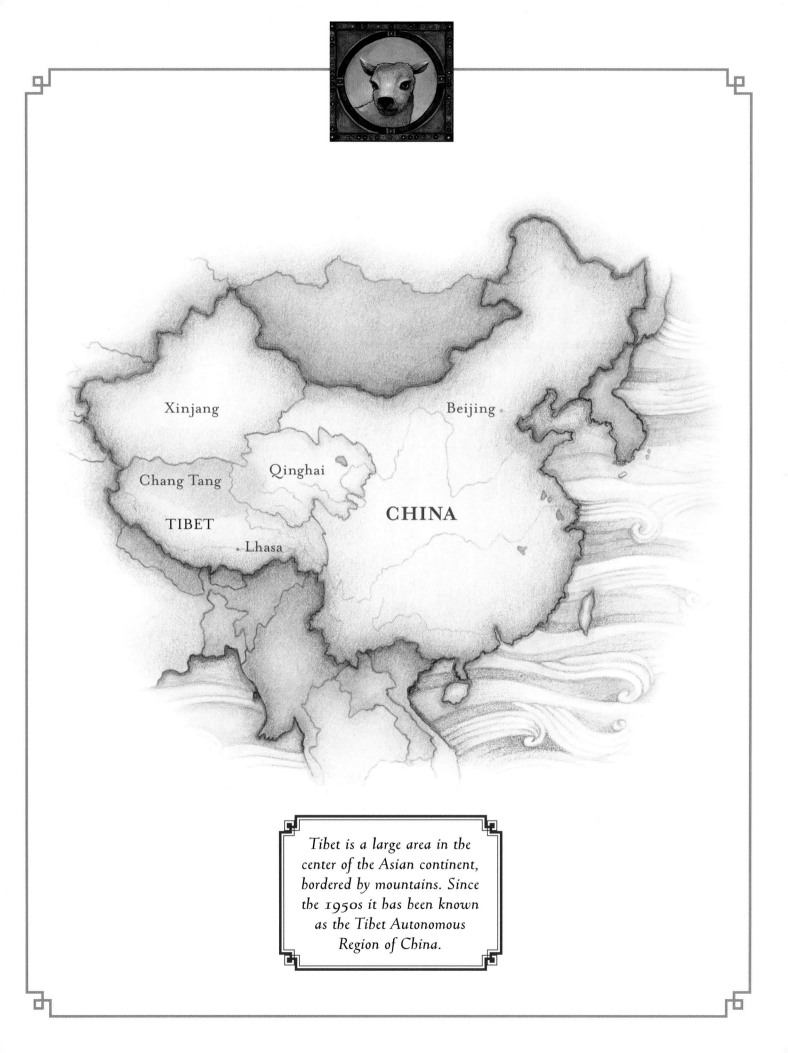

Xinjang

Beijing

Chang Tang

Qinghai

TIBET

CHINA

Lhasa

Tibet is a large area in the
center of the Asian continent,
bordered by mountains. Since
the 1950s it has been known
as the Tibet Autonomous
Region of China.

THE CHANG TANG

There is a place so cold,
it takes the fleece of five sheep to keep one person warm,
so high,
with so little rain,
the tallest tree is a shrub
that would not reach a grown man's knee.

This place is called the Chang Tang,
the northern plains of Tibet.
In this cold, windy country live the chiru.
Without the chiru (*chee-roo*)
there would be no story.

CHIRU

Chiru are the only animals of their kind.
They look like antelope
but are related to wild goats and sheep.

Chiru males have long black horns that might be taken for a
moving forest of tree branches when a group passes by.
Many Tibetans believe these horns
have special healing powers.

*From hoof to shoulder,
chiru are about as tall
as baseball bats.*

The chiru are also special for this:

Each summer, across the Chang Tang,
chiru females migrate in large groups
to faraway, secret areas to give birth.
Where are these secret places?
For hundreds of years,
even Tibetan nomads did not know.

Chiru wool is special, too—the warmest and finest in the world.
People call it shahtoosh, the king of wools.

Shawls made of shahtoosh are elegant, soft, and warm.
When wealthy women in the cities of the world
discovered these shawls,
chiru across the Chang Tang were killed for their wool.
The population shrank from one million chiru
to fewer than one hundred thousand.

In the wide, unpeopled plains,
who would care if the chiru disappeared?

Without George B. Schaller
there would be no story.

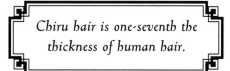

*Chiru hair is one-seventh the
thickness of human hair.*

GEORGE B. SCHALLER

When George Schaller was a boy in Germany
he read books about Tibet and imagined himself
on the high plains.
When he grew up, he traveled the world studying wildlife
and made many trips to Tibet,
where he worked with Tibetan and Chinese scientists.

George Schaller was sure that if the chiru were not protected,
they would soon be extinct. Gone: nothing
left but bones and black horns.

He believed the secret place
where the Chang Tang chiru gave birth
must be protected from hunters.
But first he had to find this place.
He decided to follow the thousands of chiru
who would begin walking north
toward the Kunlun Mountains in late May.

Why can't chiru be sheared, as sheep are?
They would freeze in their cold climate without
their wool. They have, so far, not survived
in captivity, so cannot be raised for their wool.

But he arrived too late.
The chiru had already left.

The next spring he arrived in time, but travel was slow.
His trucks got mired in snow and mud.
He ran short of food and fuel and had to turn back.
The year he took camels and donkeys
he got closer to the secret calving area,
but had to turn back when food ran out
for the pack animals.

Still the chiru were being killed—thousands each year.
George Schaller wrote,
"Wearing a shahtoosh shawl is the same
as wearing three to five dead chiru."

That's when four mountain-climbing men offered to help.
They would take no trucks to get stuck,
no camels or donkeys to feed.
They would be the pack animals themselves, and follow the chiru
more than two hundred miles to find the secret place.

Without these trekkers there would be no story.

Others were also working to save chiru.
In the eastern Chang Tang, a group of Tibetan volunteers who
called themselves the Yak Brigade apprehended many chiru poachers.
In 1994 their leader was killed by poachers. Laws were passed
in many countries making it illegal to buy or sell chiru shawls.
But the poaching continued.

THE MOUNTAIN-CLIMBING MEN

These four men
have walked up the world's tallest peaks,
and kayaked the coldest seas.
They've taken photographs of places
seen mostly by high-flying birds.

But for this one summer
they did not climb mountains
or take pictures from treetops.

They pulled wheeled carts—
carts loaded with tents, cameras, journals,
water, food, and a cookstove—
across the plains of the Chang Tang.

They were carrying questions, too.
Had they brought enough food?
Would they be able to find the chiru?

Aluminum carts like rickshaws were specially made for this trip. With their loads, each cart weighed at least 250 pounds.

George B. Schaller had told the four men where to begin.
They learned to get up before sunrise
to travel before afternoon mudtime.
Often they awoke to snow.
For breakfast they ate hot oatmeal or granola with dried fruit.
Lunch was nuts, dried beef, and an energy bar.

For supper they cooked falafel or beans and rice.
The men also shared a thin slice of salami
and a few crumbles of Parmesan cheese.
Dessert was a cup of hot chocolate.

*"Mudtime" occurs when the sun melts
the ice in the soil above the permafrost,
the permanently frozen layer of soil.*

On the fifth day of the trek
photographer Jimmy Chin shouted,
"Animals! Hundreds of them!"
Rick Ridgeway looked through his binoculars
but saw only rocks shaped like resting chiru.

That night worries buzzed in their heads.
Were they making their cart-hauling trip too late?
Why had they seen so few chiru?
Were there enough females left
to make the migration to the birthing grounds?

On the sixth day,
after they unhooked their heavy carts to make camp,
photographer Galen Rowell climbed a ridge
and looked out over the plain.
He signaled, *Come quietly*.
The others crawled toward him, not saying a word.
When they looked up, they saw chiru!
A hundred chiru!

For the next four days they followed chiru
along ruts made by centuries of migrations.
When the plains led into hills
the animals spread out, taking many different paths.

The best route the trekkers could see on their maps
took them into a rough, rock-strewn canyon
with high, steep walls.

They worked together, often standing in a canyon stream—
icy water filling their boots—
pushing, pulling, lifting the heavy carts over boulders.
Rocks as big as basketballs fell off the canyon walls.

Conrad Anker touched his forehead with a photograph of his family,
as Tibetans do, to bring good luck—
luck to get them out of the canyon, luck to find the chiru again.

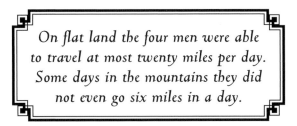

*On flat land the four men were able
to travel at most twenty miles per day.
Some days in the mountains they did
not even go six miles in a day.*

After several days in this rough canyon, the carts began to crack.
To save them from breaking, the men
backpacked their goods around the canyon rocks.

On the fifteenth day of their journey they trudged
out of the "Gorge of Despair,"
mended the carts with tape and wire,
reloaded, and pulled into the high desert.

Day sixteen: they pushed on—four alone under the huge sky.
They were always hungry and dreamed of ice cream.

Then they noticed tracks—camel tracks!
George Schaller's tracks from last year, saved in the dried mud.
And they walked faster.

At the end of that day
Rick Ridgeway thought he saw rocks in the foothills
across the plains from their campsite.
But when he looked through his binoculars, he shouted:
"Chiru! Hundreds of them. No, *a thousand!*
We've found the calving grounds!"

Galen Rowell and Jimmy Chin covered themselves with netting
and crawled on knees and elbows, just after sunrise,
to a place where they could take pictures.
These strong, bold men were quiet as new kittens
so as not to frighten the chiru
they'd come so far to find.

They went out again the next day
to take more pictures of wobbly-legged babies
running to keep up with their mothers
or flopping down to nap on the ground.

The men had not been able to haul enough food
to stay longer in the Kunlun Mountains.
But they had seen what they came for:
the secret calving grounds, the just-born chiru.
Now that they knew for sure,
and had pictures to show where it was,
George Schaller could ask the Chinese government
to make this birthing ground
a place protected from hunters forever.

The trekkers' accounts of their trip
have been carefully vague about the
exact location of the "secret place"
to help the chiru stay hidden.

CHIRU PATHS

There is a place so cold,
it takes the fleece of five sheep to keep one person warm,
so dry, the tallest tree is a shrub
that would not reach a grown man's knee.
This place is called the Chang Tang.

In this cold, windy country,
guards now patrol
for the hunters who kill for wool.

Each spring, chiru still make their trip north
to give birth,
tracing their way across the high plains,
over the steps of George B. Schaller,
over the wheel prints of the four mountain-climbing men.
When their babies are strong
the chiru walk south to home ground
over the same route.

And the story of the Chang Tang chiru circles on.

A baby chiru resting at the calving grounds in the foothills of the Kunlun Mountains.

George B. Schaller on the Chang Tang plateau in Tibet.

Female chiru on their way to the remote calving grounds in the foothills of the Kunlun Mountains.

Photo credits: Galen Rowell/Mountain Light except for center image this page, by Kay Schaller.

The four trekkers at the end of their trek to find the chiru calving grounds (left to right):
Conrad Anker, Rick Ridgeway, Galen Rowell, and Jimmy Chin. (Galen Rowell was killed in an airplane crash in California
in August 2002, just months after returning from the Chang Tang expedition.)

Trekkers work to get carts through the
"Gorge of Despair" in northern Tibet.

Author's Note

Researching this story included a trip to Aru Basin in the Chang Tang Reserve in Tibet. I'd like to thank Wellesley College for the Mary Elvira Stevens Travel Grant that made that trip possible. Ann Rider, as always, offered wise guidance and generous support during the second journey—the journey from draft to book.

I would also like to thank George B. Schaller and Rick Ridgeway for assistance with this manuscript. Their expertise is evident in many places in this story. (Quotes in the book are from The Big Open). If there are inaccuracies, they are gaps in my knowledge, not theirs.

Finally, I would like to thank these two men for the work they and their kind do. Others who share this work and whose efforts have helped save the chiru thus far include the Wildlife Trust of India; the Wildlife Crime Unit of Scotland Yard; the U.S. Fish and Wildlife Service; the Wildlife Conservation Society; the World Wildlife Fund; the International Fund for Animal Welfare; the Asia Conservation Awareness Program; the China Exploration and Research Society; and the Patagonia Clothing Company.

AMONG THE WORKS CONSULTED IN WRITING THIS BOOK ARE THE FOLLOWING:

Anker, Conrad, and David Roberts. *The Lost Explorer: Finding Mallory on Mount Everest.* New York: Simon & Schuster, 1999.

Goldstein, Melvin C., and Cynthia McBeall. *Nomads of Western Tibet.* Berkeley: University of California Press, 1990.

Ridgeway, Rick. *Below Another Sky.* New York: Henry Holt, 2000.

———. *The Big Open.* Washington, D.C.: National Geographic, 2004.

———. "275 Miles on Foot Through the Remote Chang Tang." *National Geographic* 203, no. 4 (April 2003): 104–22.

Rowell, Galen. *Mountain Light: In Search of the Dynamic Landscape.* San Francisco: Sierra Club Books, 1995.

Schaller, George B. *Tibet's Hidden Wilderness.* New York: Harry N. Abrams, 1997.

———. "Tibet's Remote Chang Tang." *National Geographic* 184, no. 2 (August 1993): 62–87.

———. *Wildlife of the Tibetan Steppe.* Chicago: University of Chicago Press, 1998.

READERS WHO WANT TO HELP CHIRU CAN SEND CONTRIBUTIONS TO

The Wildlife Conservation Society
2300 Southern Boulevard
Bronx, New York 10460
Attn: International Asia Program for Tibetan Antelope Conservation